That Summer

That Summer

David French

Talonbooks
2000

Talonbooks
P.O. Box 2076
Vancouver, British Columbia, Canada V6B 3S3
Tel.: (604) 444-4889; Fax: (604) 444-4119; Internet: www.talonbooks.com

Typeset in New Baskerville.
Printed and bound in Canada by Hignell Book Printing.

First Printing: July 2000

Talonbooks are distributed in Canada by General Distribution Services, 325
Humber College Blvd., Toronto, Ontario, Canada M9W 7C3; Tel.:(416) 213-1919;
Fax:(416) 213-1917.
Talonbooks are distributed in the U.S.A. by General Distribution Services Inc.,
4500 Witmer Industrial Estates, Niagara Falls, New York, U.S.A. 14305-1386; Tel.:1-
800-805-1083; Fax:1-800-481-6207.

Canadian Cataloguing in Publication Data
French, David, 1939-
  That summer

  A play.
  ISBN 0-88922-439-0

  I. Title.
PS8561.R44T52 2000   C812'.54   C00-910757-6
PR9199.3.F73T52 2000

The publisher gratefully acknowledges the financial support of the Canada
Council for the Arts; the Government of Canada through the Book Publishing
Industry Development Program; and the Province of British Columbia through the
British Columbia Arts Council for our publishing activities.

For Gareth, in his thirteenth year

That Summer opened the 25th Anniversary Blyth Festival season, Blyth, Ontario, on June 25, 1999 with the following cast:

MRS. CRUMP . . . . .Diana Belshaw
PAUL . . . . .Eric Davis
NARRATOR . . . . .Michelle Fisk
DAISY . . . . .Samantha Reynolds
CAITLIN . . . . .Erin Roulston
MAGGIE . . . . .Adrienne Wilson
JACK .Larry Yachimec

Directed by Bill Glassco
Set and Costume Design by Shawn Kerwin
Lighting Design by Renee Brode
Sound by Evan Turner

'O world! O life! O time!'
—Shelley

CHARACTERS

MARGARET RYAN, narrator, 49
CAITLIN, her granddaughter, 13
MARGARET RYAN, 17
DAISY RYAN, 16
JACK RYAN, 43
MRS. CRUMP, 57
PAUL WYATT, 19

The action takes place at Willow Beach, a summer resort on Wolf Lake in southern Ontario. Time present is 1990. Time past is 1958.

PRODUCTION NOTES

The production of the play should be poetic or lyrical. Accordingly, walls are not required. The cottage can be represented simply by a table and chairs. Other locations can be established the same way, or simply through light and sound.

The staging should be fluid, filmic, at moments even dream-like. As the NARRATOR recalls the summer of 1958, she wanders around the periphery of the action, watching the events unfold, reacting to her former self and the other characters.

Act I

Darkness.

Music. a distant choir sings the hymn, 'Blessed Assurance'.

The lights come slowly up on a corner of an old country churchyard. A few headstones. A white birch ... A woman kneels before a grave. This is MARGARET RYAN, who from now on will be referred to as the NARRATOR.

It is Saturday, May 26, 1990.

The NARRATOR reacts to the hymn. Then smiles at the audience.

NARRATOR:

Listen. Choir practice ... The Reverend Raymond Scott used to be the minister here at the Willow Beach Baptist Church. My sister Daisy and his son Tim took a shine to each other in the summer of 1958. The cottage we rented that year is just down there by the lake. Our neighbour was Mrs. Crump. This is her grave.

It's been thirty-two years since I was last here on Wolf Lake, though I've often returned in dreams. In truth, I wouldn't have come here this Memorial Day weekend except for my grand-daughter Caitlin. She's heard me mention this place so often that she insisted I bring her.

CAITLIN:

(*off*) Gran!

NARRATOR:

That's her now. She's thirteen.

CAITLIN enters, carrying a freshly-picked bunch of wildflowers.

CAITLIN:

I like it here, Gran. It's so peaceful, isn't it? Know what it reminds me of? The Congregational Church cemetery back home.

NARRATOR:

I suppose it does ... For me, though, it's always been unique. Don't tell anyone, but I lost my virginity one night in this graveyard. Right under that white birch.

CAITLIN:

You never mentioned that before, Gran.

NARRATOR:

It's not something a lot of seventeen-year-olds did in those days, either. Girls *or* boys ... He seemed much older, of course, your grandfather. All of nineteen.

CAITLIN:

Did you love him, Gran?

NARRATOR:

Paul? Very much ... Here, let me take those.

CAITLIN:

I just picked them.

NARRATOR:

On second thought, I can't put white lilacs on her grave. Mrs. Crump considered all white flowers unlucky …

CAITLIN:

(*reads the epitaph*)
Kathleen Crump
Born March 11, 1901
Died August 2, 1958

NARRATOR:

(*to the audience*) She drowned the summer we were here. She was fifty-seven years of age, which doesn't seem that old to me now, although it certainly did at the time.

CAITLIN:

Kathleen's such a lovely name, isn't it, Gran? Kathleen with a 'k.'

NARRATOR:

Yes, it is. Caitlin, of course, is the Gaelic form of it.

CAITLIN:

I know. I'm named after her.

NARRATOR:

Come to think of it, I didn't learn her given name till after she died. She was always Mrs. Crump to Daisy and me. No one called her Kathleen, not even my dad.

In the distance comes the muffled roll of thunder. The light changes, and a slight wind rustles the white birch.

NARRATOR:
> (*to CAITLIN*) Could be a storm brewing ... Why don't you wait in the car, Caitlin? I won't be long.

CAITLIN:
> I'd sooner poke around, Gran.

NARRATOR:
> Suit yourself. I saw some Touch-me-nots in the woods over there. And Starflowers. There used to be a sundial out on the point.

CAITLIN:
> A sundial? Really?

NARRATOR:
> No one knows who put it there. The woods have probably claimed it by now.

CAITLIN:
> I'll find it. Thanks, Gran. (*She exits*)

NARRATOR:
> Back in the 1950s, my dad was the guidance counselor at our local high school. We lived in Vermont, in a small town called Jericho, our clapboard house not far from the Congregational Church.
>
> When my mom was alive, our family spent the summers on Cape Cod. But after she died, and

Dad married Sally, we'd drive to Old Orchard Beach in Maine.

However, 1958 was different. That spring, Sally began an affair with our life insurance salesman. And when Dad found out, he reacted as only Dad could. He sat down and wrote Mr. Rush an angry letter, cancelling our policy. Then he rented the cottage up here on Wolf Lake in southern Ontario.

His plan, I suppose, was to separate the moon-struck lovers. Maybe bring Sally back to her senses.

It didn't. For two weeks, Sally pouted and sulked or went for long walks. At every meal her empty chair sat there like a rebuke. And at every meal my sister Daisy would mention it ...

The lights rise on the cottage ... JACK, MARGARET, and DAISY are seated at the table, the room washed in the gold-red light of late afternoon. Even at seventeen, MARGARET has a watchful quality about her. She is flat-chested, and self-conscious, and clearly not as sociable as DAISY.

DAISY:
Dad.

JACK:
What?

DAISY:
Dad, the tension here is killing me. I think I'm getting a bleeding ulcer. And don't laugh.

JACK:

I'm not laughing, Daisy. Did you hear me laugh, Margaret?

MARGARET says nothing.

DAISY:

Dad, I think you need your eyes examined. In case you haven't noticed, Sally's not at the table. This time, Dad, she's locked herself in the bathroom. I think she's reading *Doctor Zhivago.*

JACK:

She has a splitting headache.

DAISY:

Splitting headache? Dad, she's had a splitting headache for two weeks. Either she's lying through her teeth or she has a brain tumour.

JACK:

Keep your voice down, will you? ... (*He pours himself a bourbon*)

DAISY:

One thing I know, Dad. Maggie and I couldn't refuse to come to the table, could we? (*Then*) Could we, Dad?

JACK:

Sally's a grown woman. If she wants time alone, that's her business ... Want some advice? Ignore her.

DAISY:

Ignore her? Oh, sure. That's like ignoring a hangnail.

MARGARET:

Let's face it, Dad. Sally didn't want to come here in the first place. That's why she's acting this way … Why not admit you made a mistake and send her home? …

JACK says nothing.

DAISY:

Dad?

JACK:

I can't do that, Margaret.

MARGARET:

Why not?

JACK:

I just can't.

MARGARET:

Dad, I can't believe the hold she has on you. Is it because she looks so much like Mom? Is it?

JACK:

For God's sake, Margaret, you want Sally to hear you say that? (*He belts back the bourbon*)

NARRATOR:

I noticed Dad was beginning to drink a lot. He hardly drank at all when Mom was alive.

MARGARET:

> Alright. But don't let her ruin it for the rest of us, okay? I agree with Daisy. I don't want to spend every meal like a Trappist monk.

DAISY:

> She means in silence, Dad.

JACK:

> I know what she means, Daisy.

MARGARET:

> Dad, it's summer. Daisy and I are young. I don't see why we have to tiptoe around like someone's dying in the next room.

DAISY:

> Like Garbo in *Camille*.

JACK:

> (*slams his glass on the table*) No wonder I drink!

> *Light fades on the cottage.*

NARRATOR:

> In the third week of July, it rained two days straight, and Sally became even more withdrawn, almost catatonic. And then the miracle happened. The morning the sun came out, Sally appeared for the first time in days. And somehow we knew, before being told, that Dad had agreed to send her home … As it turned out, he'd decided to drive her there himself. All the way back to Jericho …

Music: 'Blueberry Hill' by Fats Domino.
The lights come up on the front porch ...
MARGARET, in a skirt and blouse, sits on the
porch, writing in a blue hardback book. DAISY, in
a two-piece bathing suit, sits on the steps, painting
her toenails red.

NARRATOR:

That morning, Sally was all smiles. She even
insisted on carrying out her suitcases. I
remember she waited in the car, the radio on,
her copy of *Lolita* raised to her face like a
hymnal ...

MARGARET:

The world is such a mystery, isn't it, Daisy? I
mean, I can understand why Sally might be
attracted to Dad. What I can't understand is why
she'd fall for a loser like Mr. Rush. Would you
risk it all for someone like that?

DAISY:

Are you kidding? I wouldn't even buy insurance
from him. How can you trust a man who wears a
hair-piece and drives an Edsel?

MARGARET:

I know. His last car was a '56 Packard. That's just
a glorified Studebaker.

Pause.

DAISY:

You don't suppose he's a great lover, do you? A sexual acrobat?

MARGARET:

(*incredulous*) Mr. Rush?

DAISY:

Tim Scott says short guys are usually great in bed.

MARGARET:

Know why Tim says that? Because Tim Scott is five feet tall with his shoes on.

DAISY:

He is not, Maggie. He's five-foot-six, soaking wet.

MARGARET:

Maybe the truth is nobody understands why we're attracted to each other. Maybe it's all just chemistry, like fireflies. Is that possible?

JACK comes out, carrying a suitcase.

JACK:

What's that, Margaret? Is what possible?

MARGARET:

Dad, remember when you first met Mom? The year you tried out for the Boston Braves?

DAISY:

He met her the first week in Florida, didn't you, Dad? She kept giving you the eye.

JACK:

I was a goner, Daisy. From the moment I first laid eyes on her.

MARGARET:

Dad, how did you know she was *the* one? You know, the one?

JACK:

You just know it, Margaret. When it happens to you, it'll hit you like a line drive to the heart. Believe me.

The car horn sounds.

JACK:

Alright, you two, I've got to go. Now pay attention. I want you to look after each other. Daisy, you listen to your sister, you hear? Margaret, you need anything, you ask Mrs. Crump. She'll be keeping an eye on you.

DAISY:

Keeping an eye on us? What for?

MARGARET:

We're not delinquents, Dad.

JACK:

I know you're not. She'll just be dropping in now and then. See how you're coping ... Look, I'll be back as soon as possible. I promise. No more than ten days.

DAISY:

Ten days? That's a long, long time, Dad.

JACK:

I don't like it, either, sweetheart. But right now I can't help it. You see, Sally and I have … Well, we've decided to separate for a while. Don't suppose that comes as much of a shock, does it?

DAISY:

It doesn't even register on the Richter scale.

MARGARET:

Besides, the walls here are paper thin.

DAISY:

What does she expect you to do? Find an apartment for her? Help her move in?

JACK:

Don't make it harder than it is, Daisy.

MARGARET:

Dad, you know why she wants her own place, don't you? She's not fooling anyone. All of New England knows about her and Mr. Rush.

Car horn sounds.

DAISY:

Dad, promise us one thing. Promise you won't paint her stupid place? Or pick out wallpaper? Promise?

JACK:

> I promise. Cross my heart … (*He kisses DAISY*) See
> you soon. Be good, now, you two. And don't give
> Mrs. Crump a hard time.

DAISY:

> We won't.

JACK:

> (*kisses MARGARET*) Things'll be better now,
> Margaret. Much better. You'll see.

DAISY:

> 'Bye Dad. I love you.

> > *JACK walks off, carrying his suitcase.*

MARGARET:

> Drive carefully!

> > *MARGARET and DAISY stand in the yard, waving
> > at the departing car.*

NARRATOR:

> We watched them drive off. Sally wore a red
> cotton dress and Wayfarer sunglasses, her hair
> like gold in the morning sun.

MARGARET:

> Look how she ignores him.

DAISY:

> What a bitch.

NARRATOR:

Farther on, I saw my dad salute the rearview mirror. Then he struck the horn once, just once, with the heel of his hand, one long drawn-out note of goodbye. And the sleek blue Chevy, the sun glinting off the narrow chrome of its fins, took the bend in the road, away from the lake, and was gone.

DAISY:

Good riddance.

The light fades on MARGARET and DAISY.

NARRATOR:

Memory, of course, is selective. So much about that summer I've long forgotten. After all, it's been more than three decades. And yet what happened in the next week is as fresh in my mind as though it had just happened.

And besides, there are some things in life we simply don't forget. Ever.

Music: 'Red River Rock' by Johnny & the Hurricanes.

The lights rise on the churchyard ... MARGARET sits on the grass, her Yankee's baseball cap beside her. She is writing with a yellow pencil in her blue hardback book. Ironically, this is the spot that a few weeks later will be MRS. CRUMP's grave.

PAUL WYATT, runs on. He notices MARGARET who is completely unaware of his presence ... After a moment, PAUL removes an harmonica from his pocket. Rubs it on his shirt. Then blows a few notes. MARGARET, startled, scrambles to her feet, clutching her book.

PAUL:

Sorry 'bout that. Did I frighten you?

MARGARET:

Yes, you frightened me! Do you always do that? Sneak up on people? What's wrong with you? What if I had a heart condition? (*She slaps the grass off her dress*)

PAUL watches her. Finally—

PAUL:

Do you?

MARGARET:

(*looks at him*) Do I what?

PAUL:

Have a weak heart?

MARGARET:

That's not the point, stupid.

PAUL:

What is the point?

MARGARET:

Forget it. Just scram. Can't you see I want to be alone? ... Look, if you don't leave, I'll scream. I mean it.

PAUL:

Go ahead.

MARGARET:

    I will. I'll call the minister.

PAUL:

    He wouldn't hear you. He's hard at work on next week's sermon. The parable of the ten virgins. Remember that one?

MARGARET:

    No.

PAUL:

    Five were wise, four were foolish, and the tenth was wearing a baseball cap.

MARGARET:

    Very funny.

    Pause. PAUL blows on the harmonica.

MARGARET:

    Is this how you get your kicks? Lurking in graveyards? Serenading strange girls?

PAUL:

    If you ask me, you don't look all that strange. In fact, you almost look normal.

MARGARET:

    Normal? Thanks a lot. That's like calling someone cute.

PAUL:

    Actually, if I had to describe you in a word, I'd say you were …

MARGARET:
    What?

PAUL:
    I don't know. Different.

MARGARET:
    Different? You mean, peculiar?

PAUL:
    I mean, unusual. Unlike anyone else ... For one
    thing, you're not like your sister at all, are you?
    Not really.

MARGARET:
    You know my sister?

PAUL:
    I've seen you together. Mostly at the Red Pavilion
    ... She always dances with Tim Scott. You just sit
    and watch.

MARGARET:
    So? What's wrong with that?

PAUL:
    Nothing's wrong with it. Don't be so defensive.

        Pause.

MARGARET:
    I don't dance, that's all.

PAUL:
    Because you can't? Or because you won't?

MARGARET:

What difference does it make? Not every girl's like Daisy, you know. That hardly makes me neurotic.

PAUL:

I didn't say that it did.

MARGARET:

Besides, the boys here are stand-offish. Except with Daisy, that is …

PAUL:

Well, maybe you intimidate them. They probably think you don't want to dance. That's why they don't ask you.

MARGARET:

Why would they think that?

PAUL:

Are you kidding? Ever see yourself at a dance? You just sit there.

MARGARET:

So?

PAUL:

It's the way you sit. Knees together. A scowl on your face. A glass wall around you.

MARGARET:

You're crazy.

PAUL:

Am I?

MARGARET:

Anyway, the glass wall didn't keep you away, did it? Whatever your name is.

PAUL:

It's Paul. Paul Wyatt ... No, I'm dying to know what's in that book of yours ... The first time I saw you was at the Lodge. You were writing all by yourself at a corner table. I figured you must be writing your boyfriend back in Vermont.

MARGARET:

I don't have a boyfriend. Besides, how do you know where I'm from?

PAUL:

Can't keep a secret here. A Vermont licence plate is rare ... I even know your name. It's Maggie Ryan. A lovely Irish name, that.

MARGARET:

You think so? I always thought it sounded like a nun.

PAUL:

It's beautiful. Take my word for it ... So, Maggie Ryan, what's in that blue book you carry with you everywhere? Memories? Dreams? Deep, dark secrets?

MARGARET:

It's a novel, if you must know. I don't have a title yet. Not that I'd divulge it if I did.

PAUL:

A novel?

MARGARET:

It's set in Jericho, Vermont. The way Grace
Metalious set *Peyton Place* in New Hampshire.
Only my book will be even more shocking. Might
even get me kicked out of school.

PAUL:

How so?

MARGARET:

It's a sexual grenade lobbed into the strait-laced
streets of New England. BOOM!

PAUL:

So, Maggie, you know a lot about sex, do you?

MARGARET:

Enough.

PAUL:

Why? How old are you?

MARGARET:

Old enough. I'm seventeen ... Why? How old are
you? Twenty-two?

PAUL:

Twenty-two! Get serious.

MARGARET:

You probably think you look younger, don't you?
The trouble is, people never see themselves the
way they are. Not even in the mirror.

PAUL:

Won't work, Maggie. I don't have a hang-up about my age.

MARGARET:

Why should you? Twenty-two's not old.

PAUL:

Yeah, well, I don't look twenty-two. I don't even look twenty. I'm nineteen.

MARGARET:

Actually, I thought you were eighteen. Nineteen makes you older than you look ... Mind if I ask you something?

PAUL:

What?

MARGARET:

Did you follow me here?

PAUL:

Follow you? Why would I do that?

MARGARET:

It's just that I've seen you before. Last week I was out on the point. You know, beside the sundial.

PAUL:

I know. I saw you.

MARGARET:

I saw you, too. I just didn't let on.

PAUL:

I was picking mushrooms, They're all over the place out there. Chanterelles. Dead Man's Fingers. Destroying Angels. Only the Chanterelles are any good.

MARGARET:

I saw you yesterday, too. Daisy and I went to the beach, and then you came down. Not long after.

PAUL:

Willow Beach is a small place, Maggie. Our paths were bound to cross … Like today. I came here to cut the grass. I do odd jobs for Tim's dad. He's the minister.

MARGARET:

The Reverend Scott. I know.

PAUL:

When I was coming up the road just now, that's when I saw you. You were standing here beside this tree … I had the weirdest feeling. It was like I'd seen that image before. And then I realized what is was …

MARGARET:

What?

PAUL:

You probably won't believe me if I tell you. You'll just think I'm making it up.

MARGARET:

Why? What is it?

34

PAUL:

It was a dream I had two nights ago. I'd almost forgotten it.

MARGARET:

A dream?

PAUL:

Yeah. A woman in a summer dress. A long, white summer dress.

MARGARET:

Who was it?

PAUL:

Beats me. Some woman in a churchyard. This churchyard to be exact. I recognized it.

MARGARET:

Do you remember what she looked like?

PAUL:

No. In the dream I only saw her from the back ... I could see the church over there, and the white birch, and the figure of the woman in the summer dress. She was standing here beside the tree, staring off at the lake.

MARGARET:

The lake?

PAUL:

Yeah. You know, like she was waiting for something. As if she knew something were about

to happen there … What do you suppose that
means, Maggie? A dream like that? …

*MARGARET turns and stares pensively out at the
lake. So does the NARRATOR.*

Light fades on the churchyard.

NARRATOR:

At that moment, of course, I had no inkling what
that dream meant. To me, the lake was as lovely
as summer itself, glinting out there like a blue
diamond …

Music: 'At the Hop' by Danny & the Juniors.

*The lights rise on the cottage … DAISY and MRS.
CRUMP are dancing to the song on the radio.*

NARRATOR:

(*indicates MRS. CRUMP*) Mrs. Crump.

*The song ends, and MRS. CRUMP returns to the
table; lights cigar.*

DAISY:

Mrs. Crump?

MRS. CRUMP:

Mmm.

DAISY:

Can I ask you a question? A personal question?

MRS. CRUMP:

Daisy, you can ask me anything you like. If I can
answer it, I'll be only too glad to. (*She sets down
her cigar and deals a hand of cribbage*)

DAISY:

Anything at all?

MRS. CRUMP:

Anything, luv. I know how curious young people
are. Fire away.

DAISY:

Alright ... What's it like to have sex?

MRS. CRUMP:

(*blinks*) I beg your pardon?

DAISY:

What's it like to have sex?

MRS. CRUMP:

I heard you the first time ... (*She lays down her
cards, rises, and pours herself another shot of whiskey*)
Am I out of touch? Or are all sixteen-year-olds
like you?

DAISY:

I didn't know who else to talk to. All the girls I
know are virgins. And I can't very well ask my
dad, can I?

MRS. CRUMP:

I'm not so sure you can ask me, either. But since
you have ... What exactly do you want to know?

DAISY:

Is it fun?

MRS. CRUMP:

(*laughs*) Sex? Definitely not! ... What an idea!

DAISY:

Why do we do it then? If it's not fun?

MRS. CRUMP:

I've often wondered that myself. Maybe 'cause men expect it. Can't imagine why else we would.

DAISY:

You're just saying that, aren't you?

MRS. CRUMP:

Look, if you want my honest opinion, I think the sex act is vastly overrated. A necessary evil, like high-heel shoes. And just as painful ... (*She returns to the table and picks up her cards*)

DAISY:

Some women must like it, mustn't they? Kim Novak? Marilyn Monroe?

MRS. CRUMP:

I can't answer for movie stars ... One thing I can vouch for. It wasn't sex that killed my husband, it was a bolt of lightning at the fourteenth hole. Poor Gerald. He was so much better with a golf club than with his you-know-what.

DAISY:

(*delighted*) I won't tell anyone you said that!

MRS. CRUMP:

Don't mind me, luv, it's just the bourbon. One
hundred proof whiskey does that to me … (*She
studies DAISY*) By the way, why do you want to
know all this? What have you been up to, you and
Tim?

DAISY:

Nothing.

MRS. CRUMP:

You sure?

DAISY:

I swear.

MRS. CRUMP:

Ministers' kids are the worst. My sister Joyce
married a clergyman. Her daughter Connie has
inspired more sermons than Carter has liver pills.

DAISY:

Honestly, Mrs. Crump, Tim's been a perfect
gentleman. So far, anyway.

MRS. CRUMP:

Well, don't let him twist your arm. Or sweet-talk
you. Remember, Daisy, you're only sixteen once.
Whatever you do, luv, don't grow up too fast.

DAISY:

Why? How old were you, Mrs. Crump? When you
lost your virginity?

MRS. CRUMP:

> I'd rather not dredge that up, if you don't mind.
> I'll tell you one thing, though. After it happened,
> I wondered what all the fuss was about. Hardly
> made up for all that heavy breathing ... Ah,
> good. Here comes your sister.

> > *MARGARET enters, her book in one hand, her
> > baseball cap in the other. Inside her cap are the
> > mushrooms she has just picked ... Something about
> > MARGARET puts MRS. CRUMP on red alert.*

MRS. CRUMP:

> Hello there, Margaret ... What've you been doing
> all day? Picking wildflowers?

MARGARET:

> No, I walked up to the Baptist Church. It's such a
> good place to write. So peaceful.

MRS. CRUMP:

> We wondered where you were all this time.

MARGARET:

> (*shows DAISY the mushrooms*) See what I found,
> Daisy. Chanterelles. I picked them out near the
> sundial.

MRS. CRUMP:

> How do you know they're not Jack O'Lanterns?
> Jack O'Lanterns look just like Chanterelles.

MARGARET:

> No, these are edible. Someone helped me pick
> them who knows the difference.

MRS. CRUMP:

Oh? Whom might that be?

MARGARET:

Just a boy I met at the church. He works at
Somerset Lodge.

MRS. CRUMP:

Not Paul Wyatt, by any chance?

MARGARET:

Why? Do you know him?

MRS. CRUMP:

Yes, I know him. His parents used to rent a
cottage here till they divorced ... For the past few
summers Paul's worked for old Mr. Morris. Waits
on tables. Does odd jobs.

DAISY:

Is he cute, Maggie?

MARGARET:

Cute? I didn't notice.

DAISY:

I'll bet she didn't.

MRS. CRUMP:

(*to MARGARET*) A word of advice, young lady. If
you're as smart as I think you are, you'll have
nothing more to do with him. Not if you value
your good name.

MARGARET:

Why do you say that?

41

MRS. CRUMP:

> I'm a teacher, luv. I've seen boys like Paul before.
> Some girls are attracted to boys like that. They
> always get hurt in the end.

MARGARET:

> What sort of boy is that, Mrs. Crump? Anyone
> you don't approve of?

DAISY:

> Maggie.

MRS. CRUMP:

> What sort? The sort that will lead you down the
> primrose path. Ever hear the expression: he'll
> charm the pants right off you?

MARGARET:

> So?

MRS. CRUMP:

> So Paul's the literal-minded type. He hasn't
> learned it's a figure of speech.

MARGARET:

> Well, I don't know why we're even discussing this.
> I only just met him.

MRS. CRUMP:

> I'm not blind, luv. I saw the way you came in just
> now. The way you looked. The way you walked.

MARGARET:

> What way is that?

MRS.CRUMP:
Don't pretend you don't know what I mean.

MARGARET:
I don't.

MRS. CRUMP:
Maybe it's the summer, Margaret. Summer can
dazzle and bewitch us, and do it so quickly ...
The Bible doesn't say, but I'll bet it was July in
the Garden of Eden when that old snake sidled
up to poor Eve. In February, she might've spit in
his eye.

DAISY:
I like that, Mrs. Crump.

MARGARET:
Believe me, no one's dazzled or bewitched me.
Least of all someone I've only known for two
hours ... I do have a brain in my head, you know.

MRS. CRUMP:
You're forgetting, Margaret. I was a girl myself
once. When you came home just now, it was like
seeing myself at seventeen. The summer I fell
madly in love for the first time.

MARGARET:
I wish you wouldn't say things like that. I'm not
falling in love.

MRS. CRUMP:

I just don't want you to get hurt … Don't suppose he happened to mention my niece Connie, did he?

MARGARET:

Connie? No.

DAISY:

She inspired more sermons than Carter has liver pills. Right, Mrs. Crump?

MRS. CRUMP:

He's probably forgotten her by now. Connie was last year's prize. This year, it appears, he's set his sights on you.

MARGARET:

I'd hardly describe myself as a prize.

MRS. CRUMP:

Wouldn't you? Well, you *are* a prize, and don't you ever forget it. Maybe you don't realize it yet, but you're a lovely girl with a loving heart. Oh, I know how it is at your age, all those feelings churning up inside … Just don't let anyone take advantage of that, Margaret. Not the Wyatt boy or anyone else. Not ever … (*She removes a ring from her finger*) Here. I want you to have this. It's my birthstone. Take it.

MARGARET:

I can't accept that, Mrs. Crump.

MRS. CRUMP:

Of course you can. The stone is aquamarine. It'll
help you keep a cool head … Take it, I said.

MARGARET slips the ring on her finger.

MRS. CRUMP:

I thought for a time I'd give it to Daisy. But I can
see now you need it more.

DAISY:

It's always the quiet ones, isn't it?

MRS. CRUMP:

Now sit down, Margaret. There's something
about Paul that I think you ought to know. I warn
you, though, you might not want to hear it.

Light fades on the cottage.

NARRATOR:

After my chat with Mrs. Crump, I wanted nothing
more to do with Paul. In an old English novel, he
would have been considered a cad or a bounder.

That night, Tim borrowed his dad's Ford and
drove Daisy to the dance. I preferred to be
alone …

The moon was rising over Wolf Lake. From far
off came the sound of music from the Red
Pavilion …

Music: 'Listen To Me' by Buddy Holly.
The lights rise on a dock in front of the cottage …
MARGARET stands there, gazing out at the lake.
She clutches the bottle of 'Old Hickory', from which

she takes an occasional sip as she and the
NARRATOR sing along. From behind her, PAUL
steps out of the shadows. He watches her, amused.

PAUL:

Bit off key, aren't you?

MARGARET:

(*jumps*) I wish you wouldn't do that!

PAUL:

Sorry, Maggie. I keep forgetting you might be
saddled with a bum ticker.

MARGARET:

Very funny.

PAUL:

Nice night for a swim, isn't it? Even the air's
warm ... How's the water?

MARGARET:

Why? Would you like to skinny-dip? Just the two
of us? We could swim out to the raft. Dry off in
the moonlight.

PAUL:

Sounds like a great idea to me. Except for one
thing.

MARGARET:

What?

PAUL:

You can't swim, remember? I've seen you at the beach, Maggie. You always sit under that willow tree, and write.

MARGARET:

I look too skinny in a bathing suit.

PAUL:

Some guys like thin girls.

MARGARET:

Besides, you can carry me on your back. Bet you've done it before, haven't you, Paul? You're probably an old hand at it. Isn't that how they describe someone who's almost twenty? An old hand?

PAUL:

Now who's being funny?

Pause. MARGARET takes a drink, and coughs.

MARGARET:

Did you see the moon tonight, Paul? When it first appeared it was orange. Don't they call that a Hunter's Moon? Or is every night a Hunter's Moon for someone like you?

PAUL:

The Hunter's Moon is in October ... (*Indicates the bottle*) That stuff'll make you sick, you know.

MARGARET:

Mind your own business, I said.

PAUL:

It is my business, Maggie. In case you forget, we had a date at the Red Pavilion. Or don't you remember?

MARGARET:

I changed my mind.

PAUL:

Why?

MARGARET:

I just did.

PAUL:

What am I supposed to have done? Or don't you think I deserve an explanation?

MARGARET:

What's wrong, Paul? Haven't you ever been stood up before?

PAUL:

Why would you want to stand me up? Correct me if I'm wrong, but didn't we sort of hit it off today? Isn't that why we agreed to meet at the dance?

MARGARET:

What if it was?

PAUL:

I saw your sister there. She told me she didn't know where you were ... Anyway, I came looking for you. All the lights were on at the cottage ...

MARGARET:

How did you know I was down here?

PAUL:

I could hear you singing ... Never would have taken you for a Buddy Holly fan. Billie Holiday, maybe.

MARGARET:

Shows how little you know me, Paul. How little we know each other. We probably don't have the slightest thing in common, do we?

PAUL:

Like what?

MARGARET:

How should I know? ... Cars, for instance.

PAUL:

Cars?

MARGARET:

Yeah, cars. Bet you don't know how many taillights a DeSoto has?

PAUL:

A DeSoto has six taillights. Three on each side. Been that way since '56.

MARGARET:

Think you're so smart, don't you? ... Alright, what about baseball?

PAUL:

What about it?

MARGARET:

> What player's nickname is The Say Hey Kid? And who hit .500 in the 1953 World Series?

PAUL:

> That's too easy. Ask me something harder.

MARGARET:

> Yeah, sure.

PAUL:

> I'm serious.

MARGARET:

> Bull. You don't know, do you? Admit it.

PAUL:

> Shame on you, Maggie. You probably think Americans like baseball and Canadians just like hockey. Some of us like both, you know.

MARGARET:

> I think you're full of it. You just don't know, do you? That's why you're stalling.

PAUL:

> Bet me then. If I know the answer, I get a kiss. If I don't, you can shove me off the dock, shoes and all.

MARGARET:

> I really don't want to shove you off the dock, Paul.

PAUL:

> Sure you do.

MARGARET:
Alright, maybe I do. But I don't want to kiss you.

PAUL:
Sure you do.

MARGARET:
I do not. God, you take the cake. I thought Canadians were supposed to be polite and passive?

PAUL:
All except me. I'm the exception that proves the rule ... So bet me. According to you, I can't possibly win anyway.

MARGARET:
It's a waste of time.

PAUL:
Call my bluff, why don't you? Go on.

MARGARET considers.

MARGARET:
Okay, I will. But you have to get both answers right or it's no deal. Understood?

PAUL:
Understood ... Now what was that first question again? ... (*He approaches her*) ... What player's nickname is The Say Hey Kid? That right?

MARGARET:
Yes.

PAUL:

> (*takes the bottle from her and takes a swig*) Let's see.
> The Yankee Clipper is Joe DiMaggio, the Georgia
> Peach is Ty Cobb, and the Chairman of the
> Board is Whitey Ford. The Sultan of Swat is Babe
> Ruth, the Rabbi of Swat is Moe Soloman, and the
> Say Hey Kid is none other than ... than ...

MARGARET:

> You give up?

PAUL:

> A little drum roll, Maestro!

MARGARET:

> Admit you don't know.

PAUL:

> WILLIE MAYS OF WESTFIELD, ALABAMA!

MARGARET:

> (*snatches back the bottle*) Alright, you don't need to
> show off, stupid. Just answer the question ...
> Besides, the next one's tougher. Who hit .500 in
> the '53 World Series?

PAUL:

> That's easy. The Yankees beat the Dodgers that
> year. They took it in six games. Billy Martin, the
> second baseman, finished with a .500 average. He
> also hit the winning run that drove in Hank
> Bauer in the ninth. The game was 4-3.

MARGARET:

> You shit. You knew the answers all along.

PAUL:

    I warned you, didn't I? I told you to ask me
something else … (*He steps close to MARGARET. She
backs away*) Looks like we have more in common
than you thought.

MARGARET:

    I doubt it.

PAUL:

    Bet your heart's like a bird, Maggie. Fluttering
away in its cage. Knowing you're about to be
kissed.

MARGARET:

    Yeah, right.

PAUL:

    Just think. If I hadn't come by, you'd be up all
night, reciting to yourself the immortal words of
Robbie Burns:
'Sleep I can get nane
For thinking on my Dearie.'

MARGARET:

    If that's what you believe, Paul Wyatt, you really
are the most conceited boy I ever—(*PAUL kisses
her*)

    *From the Red Pavilion comes the sound of Sam
Cooke's 'You Send Me', the NARRATOR singing
along with it … During the kiss MARGARET and
PAUL begin to move, almost unconsciously, to the
song.*

PAUL:

> See, Maggie? I knew you could dance. You just lacked the confidence ... You haven't been kissed a lot, have you? I can tell.

MARGARET:

> You can? How?

> *PAUL laughs. MARGARET pulls away.*

MARGARET:

> Why? What's so funny about the way I kiss? Tell me.

PAUL:

> Nothing's wrong with it, Maggie. It's just that you kiss like a virgin.

MARGARET:

> I am a virgin, stupid.

PAUL:

> I know. What a pity.

MARGARET:

> Not every boy's like you, is he, Paul? A Lothario? A letch? A debaucher?

PAUL:

> Debaucher? Don't you think you're being slightly old-fashioned? ... It's a different world now, Maggie. The Russians have Sputnik 3 in orbit.

MARGARET:

> Don't change the subject ... I know all about you, Paul. All about Connie, Mrs. Crump's niece.

PAUL:

What about her?

MARGARET:

I know about Brenda Fisher, too. Remember
Brenda Fisher, Paul? The waitress at Somerset
Lodge? The girl you've been going steady with?

PAUL:

Who told you all that? Mrs. Crump? ... Is that
why you stood me up tonight? Because of some
bloody old gossip?

MARGARET:

Mrs. Crump is not a gossip.

PAUL:

Isn't she?

MARGARET:

No, she's not. She just doesn't like the way you
treat the opposite sex. Neither do I, if you must
know. And if that makes me quaint or Victorian,
then so be it! (*She runs off*)

PAUL:

(*to himself*) 'So be it'? (*Then*) Wait! Maggie! Let
me explain! Dammit!

Light fades on the dock.

Music: 'Hushabye' by the Mystics.

*The lights rise on the cottage ... MRS. CRUMP
stands in the yard, gazing up at the sky.
MARGARET slips into the cottage by the back way,*

sets down the whiskey bottle, then notices MRS.
CRUMP … She turns off the radio and steps
outside. MRS. CRUMP acknowledges her with a
look.

MARGARET:

Thought you'd gone to bed, Mrs. Crump.

MRS. CRUMP:

Not yet, dear. I will when Daisy gets home …
Lovely night, isn't it? The moon's so bright, it
even lights up the dock down there.

MARGARET:

I don't like being spied on, you know.

MRS.CRUMP:

I wasn't spying, Margaret. I just happened to look
out my window … When I was young, I couldn't
sleep on nights like this. The moonlight kept me
awake.

MARGARET:

My mom was like that, too.

MRS. CRUMP:

Was she?

MARGARET:

Mostly after she took sick … She'd sit out back
every chance she got. Bundle up beside the
cherry tree and watch the stars.

MRS. CRUMP:

What happened to your mother, Margaret?

MARGARET:

She died. When I was twelve. Cancer.

MRS. CRUMP:

I wondered.

MARGARET:

Her and Dad used to rock-climb. Mostly in the White Mountains of New Hampshire. Mom's favourite place was the White Horse Ledge. There's a six-hundred foot climb there called the Inferno.

MRS. CRUMP:

You thought she'd fall, didn't you?

MARGARET:

(*nods*) Funny, isn't it? Instead, she died at home on a Monday morning, watching the cherry blossoms from her bedroom window. A month shy of her thirty-fifth birthday.

MRS. CRUMP:

Death picks its own time, luv. It's own time and its own place. The way love does, I suppose.

Pause.

MARGARET:

Mrs. Crump, you know the boy you mentioned this afternoon? The one you fell in love with at seventeen? Was that your husband?

MRS. CRUMP:

My husband? Oh, no, dear, I met Gerald years later at a picture show … No, the boy I fell for that summer was Matthew Russell. His dad had just built the Red Pavilion … In those days we lived here side by side, Matt's family in this cottage, my family next door.

MARGARET:

He lived in this cottage?

MRS. CRUMP:

(*nods*) Matt had just graduated from high school that year. He was helping his dad run the dancehall … Such a handsome boy. He had a shock of ginger hair, Matt did, and the bluest eyes you ever saw. Mother used to say, 'I wish I was twenty years younger!'

MARGARET:

(*laughs*) I bet she did.

MRS. CRUMP:

We'd known each other for the longest time, Matt and I, but suddenly that summer, we knew we were in love. I don't think we ever spoke about it, it was something we just knew. Our shared secret, so to speak … I'd fall asleep at night, thinking of Matt and I'd wake up thinking of Matt. You might say he was my Morning and my Evening Star, my beloved with those blue, blue eyes … You sure you want to hear this, dear? It all happened so long ago.

MARGARET:

Please. I want to, Mrs. Crump.

MRS. CRUMP:

The summer I fell in love was the summer of 1918. The First World War was still raging in Europe, and Matt said if it wasn't over soon, he was going to enlist. And as if the War wasn't bad enough, that spring the Spanish flu had swept the world. They called it the Spanish Lady.

MARGARET:

The Spanish Lady?

MRS. CRUMP:

No plague ever killed so many in so short a time. Between twenty-five and forty million in less that a year. More than died in the Great War.
     'I had a little bird
     And its name was Enza
     I opened the window
     And in-flu-enza.'
Little girls skipped rope to that jingle … Oh, we'd all been warned, of course, but no one listened.

MARGARET:

Warned? How?

MRS. CRUMP:

Signs. Portents. In Brazil, a sailor praying to the statue of Our Lady of Consolation saw her shed a tear. In New Zealand, a nurse glanced out a window and saw a fiery cross in the sky … Of course, none of it mattered to Matt and me. Not the War, not the Spanish Lady, nothing. All that mattered was each other ... And then in September came the second and more deadly wave of the flu, and the schools closed. Which suited us just fine. It meant we had more time at the lake. However, even that was short-lived. Calvin Coolidge saw to that.

MARGARET:
Calvin Coolidge? The President?

MRS. CRUMP:
Wilson was the President then, luv. Coolidge was the Acting Governor of Massachusetts. At the time he had fifty thousand flu cases on his hands. That's how Matt and I came to be separated, my father wanted to help. He was a doctor.

MARGARET:
I see.

MRS. CRUMP:
His practice was in Toronto, and when Coolidge asked our mayor for help, Father volunteered ... The last time I saw Matt was the day we closed the cottage and drove back to the city. He was standing here in the yard, waving goodbye.

MARGARET:
And you never saw him again?

MRS. CRUMP:

> (*shakes her head*) I promised I'd write, of course. And for a time I did. And Matt wrote back in his big neat scrawl ... But then I took sick myself and almost died. And by the time I was back on my feet, it was months later.

MARGARET:

> And you hadn't heard from him?

MRS. CRUMP:

> No, not in all that time. I suppose I thought he'd just forgotten me. Things like that can happen when people are separated ... Anyway, in the spring of 1919, the Spanish Lady had all but vanished, and Father brought us home. And come the first warm weekend in June, we drove up here to the lake ... The first thing I noticed was the 'For Sale' sign on the Red Pavilion. I saw it as we drove past ... And then we pulled in here. I saw there were words printed on the door that I couldn't make out from the road.

MARGARET:

> Words?

MRS. CRUMP:

> Four words ... The cottage was all boarded up, and when I ran up the steps, I read what Matt had printed there in his big neat hand. Four simple words in shiny black paint: WE HAVE THE FLU. He'd done that, you see, to keep others away ... It was then I understood why he hadn't written. Then and only then.

MARGARET:

He'd died, hadn't he?

MRS. CRUMP:

Yes, dear, he had. Died in this very cottage. Along with his parents.

MARGARET:

All three died here?

MRS. CRUMP:

Yes, the Spanish Lady had passed this way and taken Matt with her. For the longest time she took the heart and soul of me ... There's a poem I teach called *That Summer*. By a man named Henry Treece. Don't suppose you know it?

MARGARET:

No.

MRS. CRUMP:

(*recites*)
'That year, snow came in April and again
In May, and the pony died in his harness;
But in summer, under the whitewashed trees,
A girl in a white dress gave me an apple.
I fitted my teeth in the marks her teeth
Had made; so we were one. Then dusk
Moved slowly among the trees like a blue
Smoke at night, and I cried that joy
Could come so easily, for then I knew
It must break with as little warning.'

Offstage, a car suddenly stops on the road.

MARGARET:

> That's Daisy, now.

MRS. CRUMP:

> It's not hard to tell you've been drinking,
> Margaret. I can smell it … Was that his idea?

MARGARET:

> It was mine, Mrs. Crump. And I'm not the least
> bit intoxicated.

MRS. CRUMP:

> He's not worth the heartache, you know. All the
> whiskey in the world won't change that. Nor all
> your tears.

> *A car door slams.*

DAISY:

> (*off*) 'Night, Tim!

> *The car drives away.*

MARGARET:

> You'll be happy to know I sent him packing. He
> won't be showing his face here again, Paul.

MRS. CRUMP:

> Don't bet on it, luv. Bad pennies have a habit of
> turning up.

> *Enter DAISY, holding an orchid.*

MRS. CRUMP:

> Here she comes: the Belle of the Ball. And with
> such a beautiful orchid.

DAISY:

It's called a Yellow Lady Slipper. Tim picked it in the woods.

MRS. CRUMP:

He did? I'm impressed.

DAISY:

Maggie, you should've been at the dance tonight. Someone asked me where you were. Bet you'll never guess who it was.

MRS. CRUMP:

Paul Wyatt. She knows.

MARGARET:

He came here looking for me, Daisy. I sent him away.

DAISY:

You did? Why?

MRS. CRUMP:

I think you know why, young lady.

DAISY:

But he's so cute, Maggie. Tim didn't even like me talking to him.

MRS. CRUMP:

The more I learn about Tim Scott, the more sensible he seems. Now get to bed, Daisy. It's late. You need your rest. You, too, Margaret.

DAISY:

> (*starts into the cottage*) 'Night, Mrs. Crump. See you tomorrow.

MRS. CRUMP:

> Goodnight, luv. Sleep well.

MARGARET:

> 'Night, Mrs. Crump. (*She hugs her*)

MRS. CRUMP:

> Goodnight, Margaret. Remember: keep that ring on your finger. At least till you're safely back in Jericho. (*She exits*)

> > *MARGARET goes inside. DAISY is putting the orchid in a vase ... MARGARET watches her, absently turning the ring on her finger. Finally—*

MARGARET:

> Was he alone?

DAISY:

> Was who alone?

MARGARET:

> Don't be coy. You know who: Paul ... Was he with anyone?

DAISY:

> You mean, like Brenda Fisher?

MARGARET:

> Yes, like Brenda Fisher.

DAISY:

I wouldn't know, Maggie. I wouldn't know
Brenda if I saw her ... He did dance once with a
girl. She had auburn hair.

MARGARET:

Was she pretty?

DAISY nods.

MARGARET:

Bet that was her. Mrs. Crump said she was pretty,
remember? ... I don't get it, Daisy. Why would
Paul take an interest in me? He knows I'd never
go all the way.

DAISY:

Maybe he likes you, stupid.

MARGARET:

Why?

DAISY:

What do you mean, why? What kind of question
is that to ask?

MARGARET:

Let's face it, Daisy. I'll never be like you or
Brenda. You know it, and I know it.

DAISY:

The trouble with you, Maggie, is you have an
inferiority complex a mile wide.

MARGARET:

I don't. I'm just realistic. God, I don't even have much of a figure ... So why would Paul give me a second glance? He can have any girl in Willow Beach.

DAISY:

Remember Snow White? How she lay in her glass coffin on the green hill? How she grew more beautiful every year?

PAUL appears in the yard.

MARGARET:

So?

DAISY:

So maybe Paul's like the handsome Prince. Remember how he rides by and falls in love with her? How he wakes Snow White from that long, long sleep with a kiss?

MARGARET:

The sleep of innocence? Is that what you mean, Daisy?

DAISY:

Exactly. The sleep of innocence.

PAUL:

Maggie Ryan!

DAISY:

Did you hear that?!

PAUL:

Come out, Maggie!

DAISY:

I think I'm psychic!

MARGARET:

Tell him I'm not here.

DAISY:

(*shouts*) She's not here! Go away!

> *MARGARET switches off the lights, leaving the*
> *cottage dark except for the wash of moonlight. The*
> *porch light remains on ... MARGARET and DAISY*
> *stand motionless, listening.*

PAUL:

I know you're in there, Maggie. I can hear you
breathing. I can even hear the beating of your
heart.

DAISY:

Does he always talk like that? That's fantastic!

PAUL:

I wanted to explain, Maggie, but your temper got
the better of you. You do have a temper, you
know.

DAISY:

He's right, you do.

MARGARET:

Shh.

PAUL:

Why do you think I left the dance early tonight? Why do you think I came straight here? ... The truth is I can't get you out of my mind.

DAISY:

Say something. If he doesn't shut up, Mrs. Crump will be over here.

MARGARET:

I know. I have to get rid of him ... Go on to bed, Daisy. I can handle Paul.

DAISY:

You sure?

MARGARET:

I'm positive. Go.

> *DAISY exits ... MARGARET approaches the screen door.*

PAUL:

(*recites 'Ay Waukin, O'*)
'Simmer's a pleasant time,
Flow'rs of ev'ry colour;
The water rins o'er the haugh,
And I long for my true lover!
(*Dances playfully*)
Ay waukin, O
Waukin still and wary:
Sleep I can get nane,
For thinking on my Dearie.'

MARGARET:

> (*through the screen door*) No wonder you like Robbie Burns, Paul. He slept with half the women in Scotland.

PAUL:

> Lucky him.

MARGARET:

> How many hearts have you broken? Or have you lost count?

PAUL:

> You shouldn't listen to Mrs. Crump, you know. According to her, I make Burns look like a late bloomer.

MARGARET:

> So?

PAUL:

> Dammit, Maggie, take what she says with a grain of salt. Just 'cause I dated her niece doesn't make me the Devil, does it?

MARGARET:

> Did you sleep with Connie?

PAUL:

> I didn't deflower her, if that's what you mean. You like words like that, don't you? Deflower?

MARGARET:

> (*steps out on the porch*) What about Brenda Fisher? Shouldn't you be dallying with her right now? Instead of wasting your time with me?

PAUL:

> Dallying?

MARGARET:

> Don't make fun of me.

PAUL:

> Am I wasting my time?

MARGARET:

> You don't listen, do you? Anyone else would have gotten the message.

PAUL:

> You don't mean that, Maggie. I knew you were glad to see me tonight. Know how I knew that?

MARGARET:

> How?

PAUL:

> The way your eyes lit up. The way you kissed me.

MARGARET:

> *I* didn't kiss you, Paul Wyatt. *You* kissed *me*, remember?

PAUL:

> Let's not split hairs.

MARGARET:

It won't happen again, either. Just in case you think otherwise. (*She runs inside and snaps off the porch light*)

PAUL:

The summer's still young, Maggie. Young and green like us.

MARGARET:

Goodnight, Paul. (*Inside the cottage, MARGARET stands motionless*)

NARRATOR:

That night, I stood in the dark, listening to my breathing. I could even hear the pounding of my heart ...

PAUL:

(*sings 'A Red, Red Rose'*)
'My luve is like a red, red rose,
That's newly sprung in June:
My luve is like a melodie,
That's sweetly play'd in tune.
As fair art thou, my bonnie lass,
So deep in luve am I,
And I will luve thee still, my dear
Till a' the seas gang dry.'

> *DAISY appears in the moonlight. MRS. CRUMP appears at a distance ... MARGARET steps out onto the porch. She watches PAUL.*

PAUL:

Moonlight becomes you, Maggie Ryan. Has
anyone ever told you that before?

MARGARET:

No. As a matter of fact, no one ever has till now.

PAUL:

(*sings*)
'Till a' the seas gang dry, my dear,
And the rocks melt wi' the sun:
And I will luve thee still, my dear
While the sands o' life shall run.
(*He turns and sings the remaining lines to the
NARRATOR*)
And fare-thee-weel, my only luve,
And fare-thee-weel, a while!
And I will come again, my luve,
Though it were ten-thousand mile.'

Blackout.

Act II

Darkness.

The lights rise on the NARRATOR. She stands looking out at the lake.

NARRATOR:

(*to the audience*) Islands are so intriguing, aren't they? There's one out there in the lake. On it are the ruins of a house. I was told a murder took place there many years ago. And every summer, a scarlet flower called the Maltese Cross rises from the cracks in those stained and broken stones—on the exact spot the murder occurred.

Oh, I know the cynics will probably laugh. Or roll their eyes. The mystical dimension of life, they say, is for people like Mrs. Crump. Or poets.

I wonder. The dream that Paul had that summer—the dream of something impending—eventually came to pass on August 2nd. No one's ever explained that to me, not even in a world of quantum physics.

Just this spring, Caitlin showed me a poem by Yeats, *A Dream of Death*. The lines reminded me of that long ago summer:

'She was more beautiful than thy first love
This lady by the trees.'

Music: 'Only You' by the Platters.

The lights rise on the woods … In the dappled shade, MARGARET sits on a blanket, PAUL's head in her lap. Now and then, PAUL takes a sip of Scotch from a silver flask ... Nearby is a straw picnic basket and the remains of a lunch.

MARGARET:
Henry James thought 'summer afternoon' were the two most beautiful words in English. What do you think the most beautiful are?

PAUL:
Brigitte Bardot. Or is that French?

MARGARET:
Be serious ... You must have favourite words, don't you? And don't say 'sex'.

PAUL:
I wasn't going to.

MARGARET:
What, then?

NARRATOR:
Apple.

PAUL:
(*thinks*) Apple.

MARGARET:
Apple? That's it? Of all the words in the English language, you have to pick 'apple'?

PAUL:
I don't know all the words in English, Maggie. And listen, if you don't want to know my

favourite words, don't ask me. *(He reaches up, draws MARGARET's face down, and kisses her)*

MARGARET:
(*breaks free*) What else?

PAUL:
Awl.

MARGARET:
Spell it.

PAUL:
A-w-l. It's a tool for punching holes in wood or leather. Carpenters use it, and shoemakers. I like words like that. Words you can rap your knuckles on … (*Playfully*) Another word I like is syphilis. I like the sound of it. And gonorrhea. That also drips.

MARGARET:
I'm sorry I asked.

PAUL pulls her down on the blanket.

PAUL:
(*kisses her eyes*) Eyes. (*Nose*) Nose. (*Lips*) Lips. (*Throat*) Throat. All perfectly good words … But not as good as 'bellybutton'. (*He tries to kiss her there, but she grips his hair from the back*) Ouch!

MARGARET:
(*sits up*) Well, behave yourself.

PAUL:

Bet I know your favourite words, Maggie. Those two old spinsters who guard the Sacred Grove: Maidenhead and Chastity.

MARGARET:

Well, you know I don't like you doing that. I must've told you a hundred times.

PAUL:

I didn't know you were keeping count.

MARGARET:

Besides, it's not that I don't like it, Paul, it's just that ...

PAUL:

What?

MARGARET begins to clean up the picnic lunch, folding the cloth napkins and putting away the cutlery and paper plates.

MARGARET:

Well, if it's too frustrating for you, maybe we oughtn't to see each other. Maybe it's not such a good idea.

PAUL:

I can't believe you said that.

MARGARET:

I mean it.

PAUL:

No, you don't. You know damn well I don't want to be with Brenda. That's why I broke up with her ... You don't have to keep testing me.

MARGARET:

She's not what I expected, you know. She's even prettier than I thought ... I have a confession to make, Paul. I went to the Lodge the other day. Just to see what she looked like.

PAUL:

Oh?

MARGARET:

You and Mr. Morris were mending the tennis net ... Are you mad?

PAUL:

No, I'm flattered.

MARGARET:

I only just peeked in. Brenda was waiting on someone. I don't think she saw me.

PAUL:

If she had, I'd know. She's always making snide little comments.

MARGARET:

Like what?

PAUL:

Oh, you know. How I'll never see you again after Labour Day. How I'm just using you to kill time. Things like that.

MARGARET:

> What do you say to her?

PAUL:

> I tell her she's full of it. I say I'm driving down to
> Vermont in the fall. How I have it all mapped
> out.

MARGARET:

> Interstate 89.

PAUL:

> Not far from Burlington. She doesn't believe me.
> She thinks it's just a summer romance ... Is
> 'summer romance' better that 'summer
> afternoon'?

MARGARET:

> We'll send her a postcard of Mt. Mansfield. That
> should convince her. Oh, Paul, I can't wait to
> show you Jericho. The gorge ... the old mill ...
> the drugstore I hang out at. The man who owns
> it, Mr. Prince, looks just like Officer Frank Smith,
> Jack Webb's partner on Dragnet. We had our
> own celebrity once. W.A. Bentley, the Snowflake
> King.

PAUL:

> The Snowflake King?

MARGARET:

> The world's foremost authority on snowflakes.
> He photographed fifty-three hundred of them.
> The largest collection of its kind in the world.

PAUL:
    I'm impressed.

MARGARET:
    I can tell.

PAUL:
    No, I am. Canadians look forward to snow. It's in
    our blood, like hockey.

MARGARET:
    You're awful.

PAUL:
    Wonder why a man spends his life
    photographing snowflakes? Is it the elegance
    of the structure that appeals to him? Or its
    transitory nature? Or maybe old W.A. was really
    a poet at heart. Like Robbie Burns.
        'But pleasures are like poppies spread—
        You seize the flow'r, its bloom is shed;
        Or like the snow falls in the river—
        A moment white—then melts for ever.'

    He kisses her.

MARGARET:
    Paul?

PAUL:
    What?

MARGARET:
    Do you love me?

PAUL:

You know I do.

MARGARET:

Say it. I like to hear you say it.

PAUL:

I love you.

MARGARET:

I love you, too ... Maybe those are the three most
beautiful words in any language.

NARRATOR:

'I love you.'

PAUL:

Maybe so.

MARGARET:

I can't believe it's happened so fast. Sometimes I
want to pinch myself. It's like I'm dreaming ...
Funny how Mrs. Crump knew, isn't it?

PAUL:

Knew what?

MARGARET:

She said I'd fallen for you the first day we met. I
guess I didn't want to admit it, not even to myself
... She said something else, too.

PAUL:

What?

NARRATOR:

Summer is a time of magic.

MARGARET:

She said summer was a time of magic. A time of enchantment. I suppose that's true, isn't it? It's always the summers we remember in our lives ... Paul?

PAUL:

Mmm?

MARGARET:

Would you do something for me if I asked you to? Would you Paul? It would mean a lot to me.

PAUL:

What?

MARGARET:

Make up with her.

PAUL:

She tried to break us up, remember?

MARGARET:

I want us all to be friends, Paul. I want us to have dinner together.

PAUL:

She might not feel the same. Especially after what happened last year ... I didn't tell you this, Maggie, but she walked in one day and caught Connie and me fooling around.

MARGARET:
    Mrs. Crump caught you and her niece?

PAUL:
    Stark naked.

MARGARET:
    Paul!

PAUL:
    I know.

MARGARET:
    What did she do?

PAUL:
    Took the flyswatter to us ... The next day she put
    Connie on the bus back to the city. Wasn't much
    she could do to me. My folks were in summer
    stock.

MARGARET:
    Wait a minute ... Your parents are actors? Mrs.
    Crump didn't tell me that.

PAUL:
    They're good actors, too. For years, they
    pretended to be in love ... My mother lives now
    with someone half her age, and my dad has this.
    (*He indicates the flask*) He did a one-man show on
    Burns last winter. Took it on tour. I used to run
    lines with him. That's how come I know old
    Robbie, in case you were wondering.
        'A man may drink and no be drunk
        A man may fight and no be slain;'

NARRATOR:

> 'A man may kiss a bonnie lass,
> And aye be welcome back again.'

MARGARET:

Promise me you'll come to dinner? Promise?
(*And with that, she runs off*)

The lights fade slowly on the woods.

NARRATOR:

Mrs. Crump. We hadn't known her that long,
Daisy and me, but already she was like a mother
to us. More of a mother than Sally. That's why I
invited her and Paul to dinner. I wanted them to
become close.

Looking back now, I can see that I wanted
something else as well: her blessing.

Meanwhile, Daisy had her own problems—
problems which threatened to upset the apple
cart ...

Music: 'Come Softly To Me' by the Fleetwoods.
The lights rise on the cottage. It is early evening
... DAISY is alone on stage.

MARGARET:

(*off*) Daisy, don't forget to set out the candles ...
Daisy, did you hear what I said? ...

MARGARET appears, putting on earrings.

MARGARET:

Are you sure you're okay?

DAISY:

> I wish you'd quit asking me that. I told you
> before, I'm alright. Don't bug me.

MARGARET:

> Paul and Mrs. Crump will be here any minute.
> You want them to see you like this? ... Now
> whatever happened between you and Tim, I'm
> sure it's not that serious. So why don't you just
> call him? You know you're going to anyway.

DAISY:

> How can I call him, Maggie? We don't have a
> phone, remember?

MARGARET:

> I know that ... I must be losing my mind.

DAISY:

> Besides, I wouldn't call Tim Scott after last night,
> not if he was James Dean! I hate him! (*She drops
> onto a chair, heartbroken*)

MARGARET:

> Daisy, I don't have time for this. Not now ... (*She
> switches off the radio*) Look, maybe you're just
> homesick. Or maybe you miss Dad. Don't forget,
> he's supposed to be back soon.

DAISY:

> It's not Dad I miss, it's Tim. And I'm not
> homesick, either. I'm sixteen years old. I'm not a
> baby.

MARGARET:

Alright, tell me what happened. It can't be that bad.

DAISY:

We broke up, Tim and me.

MARGARET:

He doesn't want to see you anymore?

DAISY:

No.

MARGARET:

But I thought you two were getting along?

DAISY:

We were. Sort of.

MARGARET:

Everybody has a spat now and then. Even the best of friends.

DAISY:

It's not a *spat*, Maggie. And it's not a *snit*, either. God, the words you use!

MARGARET:

What happened, then? Tell me.

DAISY:

If I do, will you promise not to tell Dad? He mustn't find out. It would kill him.

MARGARET:

Daisy, what have you done?

DAISY:

Nothing. Don't look at me like that.

MARGARET:

It's not what I think, is it? Tell me it isn't, Daisy.

DAISY:

Why? What do you think it is?

MARGARET:

You tell me.

DAISY:

I can't. I can't say it.

MARGARET:

Did you, Daisy?

DAISY:

What?

MARGARET:

Did you? I want to know.

DAISY:

Not exactly.

MARGARET:

Not exactly? What does that mean? Either you
did it with Tim or you didn't do it with Tim. Now
which is it?

DAISY:

I didn't do it with Tim.

MARGARET:

> I don't believe you … Now what happened last
> night? And don't lie to me.

DAISY:

> Alright … Tim suggested we go out on the lake.
> You know, in his dad's row-boat … It was so
> beautiful, Maggie. So quiet out there. We just lay
> in the boat and looked at the stars. The moon
> was over MacGregor's Island.

MARGARET:

> You lost your virginity in a row-boat?

DAISY:

> It has a flat bottom.

MARGARET:

> Daisy, how could you? Don't you know what
> might have happened out there? Don't you?

DAISY:

> I can swim.

MARGARET:

> I'm not talking about tipping over. I meant …
> Oh, God, Daisy, don't you remember what
> happened to Norma Potter last winter? She was
> sent to Missouri to look after her aunt. Everyone
> knew she had no Aunt Trixie in Kansas City.

DAISY:

> We were just lying there, and things got out of
> hand, I guess. All of a sudden he was inside me,
> and I said, 'No Tim! No!' and I pushed him off

... He wasn't in very far, Maggie. Just a little. And only for a second or two. Does that mean I'm technically still a virgin?

MARGARET:

I don't know, Daisy. I'm not much of an expert ... Did you bleed?

DAISY:

Bleed? No.

MARGARET:

Then you're probably still a virgin.

DAISY:

He makes me feel like there's something wrong with me. Like I'm a cold fish. Do you think I'm a cold fish, Maggie?

MARGARET:

That sounds more like me, don't you think?

DAISY:

I wish I could quote the Bible at him, but I don't know it that well. It probably wouldn't impress him anyway. His dad's a minister, but Tim can't even quote John 3:16. 'For God so loved the world ... '

MARGARET:

Do you flirt with him Daisy? You shouldn't, you know. You can get yourself in trouble that way.

DAISY:

    I know. Tim says there's a ten-letter word for girls who like to tease.

MARGARET:

    Want to know what I'd do, Daisy? If I were you, I mean?

DAISY:

    I know what you're going to say.

MARGARET:

    What?

DAISY:

    You're going to say I should forget him. That he doesn't respect me … That's what Dad would say.

MARGARET:

    Respect is important.

DAISY:

    But I love him, Maggie.

MARGARET:

    If he loved you, too, he wouldn't treat you like that. He's only thinking of himself.

DAISY:

    Oh, sure. As if Paul doesn't want to get you into bed. Boy, Maggie, are you naive.

MARGARET:

    I'm not saying Paul doesn't want to. I'm saying he doesn't make me feel as if I have to. And so far he hasn't laid a hand on me.

MRS. CRUMP appears in the yard, smoking a cigar.
She drops the butt on the ground and steps on it.
Then she hurries inside the cottage.

MRS. CRUMP:
    I want you girls to promise me you'll never take
    up smoking. Cigars are harder to quit than sex.
    Oh, my. Look at the two of you.

MARGARET:
    What?

MRS. CRUMP:
    You're both so pretty tonight. I wish I'd brought
    along my camera ... (*Suddenly she notices the vase
    of wildflowers on the table*) Oh, my Lord. Look.

DAISY:
    What?

MRS. CRUMP:
    Queen Anne's Lace. Don't you girls know that
    white flowers are deemed unlucky?

DAISY:
    They are?

MRS. CRUMP:
    Omens of death ... Never bring white flowers
    inside the house. Especially those with a strong
    scent. Like lilies-of-the-valley or white lilacs.

MARGARET:
    Queen Anne's Lace have no scent, Mrs. Crump.

91

MRS. CRUMP:

> True, dear. But they're still white, aren't they? And we don't want to tempt Fate, now do we? ... (*She carries the vase outside and tosses away the offending flowers*)

DAISY:

> If white flowers can flip her lid, wait'll she finds out who's coming to dinner.

MRS. CRUMP:

> (*returning*) There. The wood lilies are just as lovely on their own. (*She sets down the vase and arranges the flowers*)

MARGARET:

> Don't you think you're overreacting, Mrs. Crump?

MRS. CRUMP:

> Overreacting? Oh, no, luv. There are strange forces at work in life. Just because we can't explain them doesn't mean they don't exist. Why, look at my husband. The night before he died, a black dog paid us a visit. Sat in front of our home in Toronto and cried his eyes out. The next morning he was struck by lightning.

MARGARET:

> The dog was struck by lighting?

DAISY:

> Not the dog, Maggie. Mr. Crump.

MARGARET:

Oh.

MRS. CRUMP:

The same man who stormed the beach at
Dieppe, and not a scratch on him ... Yes, he went
to play golf that day and forgot his amulet. Don't
suppose you know the difference between an
amulet and a talisman, do you?

MARGARET:

No, I don't.

MRS. CRUMP:

Well, an amulet's supposed to protect you,
Margaret. Like that ring I gave you. A talisman
just brings you luck ... Poor Gerald. He might be
alive today if he hadn't walked off without that
shark's tooth. He carried it all through the war.
Wore it later on his watch-chain.

> *PAUL enters the yard and knocks on the door ...*
> *MARGARET and DAISY exchange a look.*

MRS. CRUMP:

(*to MARGARET*) Better get that, luv. Someone's at
the door.

MARGARET:

I know. I meant to tell you, Mrs. Crump, but ...
Well, I sort of invited someone else to dinner
tonight. A friend.

MRS. CRUMP:

Oh? Whom might that be, Margaret?

MARGARET:
Paul Wyatt.

MRS. CRUMP:
Let me get this straight, luv. You invited the Wyatt boy to dinner and it slipped your mind? Just like that?

MARGARET:
Why? Don't you believe me?

MRS. CRUMP:
Are you forgetting I'm a teacher? I've heard lies that deserve a Pulitzer. That one doesn't even make the Hit Parade.

DAISY:
Can't you give him a second chance, Mrs. Crump? For Maggie's sake? Can't you?

MARGARET:
Maybe he's changed, Mrs. Crump. Maybe you won't even recognize him.

MRS. CRUMP:
Not if he keeps his Jockeys on I won't.

A second knock on the door.

MARGARET:
I like Paul, Mrs. Crump. I want you to remember that. (*She lets PAUL in*)

MRS. CRUMP:
Alright, luv, I'll be as good as gold. I promise. (*To DAISY*) Not that she deserves it, mind.

MARGARET:

   (*to PAUL*) Hi.

PAUL:

   Hi, Maggie. Hi, Daisy.

DAISY:

   Hi, Paul.

MRS. CRUMP:

   Hello there, Paul.

PAUL:

   Hello, Mrs. Crump.

MRS. CRUMP:

   Funny, I almost said, 'I haven't seen that much of
   you this summer.' But I suppose that could be
   taken the wrong way, couldn't it?

DAISY:

   Mrs. Crump, you promised!

MRS. CRUMP:

   I know. I can't be trusted.

   Pause.

MARGARET:

   Why don't we all sit down? Dinner won't be ready
   for a while yet … (*DAISY and PAUL sit*) Can I get
   you a drink, Mrs. Crump? Bourbon?

MRS. CRUMP:

   Bourbon would certainly hit the spot, Margaret.

MARGARET:

A double?

MRS. CRUMP:

A double would be a bull's eye. (*She lights a cigar*)

MARGARET pours the whiskey.

MARGARET:

Paul, why don't you tell Mrs. Crump what your folks are doing this summer?

PAUL:

My folks? ...

DAISY:

His dad's in *Charley's Aunt* in Muskoka. And his mom's in *The Seagull* in Philadelphia.

MARGARET:

What part is she playing, Paul? I forget.

PAUL:

Polina.

DAISY:

Do you know the play, Mrs. Crump?

MRS. CRUMP:

I most certainly do ... Poor Polina. Married to that wretched man, the years piling up around her like dust. It's tragic.

PAUL:

Didn't Chekhov called *The Seagull* a comedy?

MRS. CRUMP:

    A comedy? Only a Russian would find those
    people funny.

PAUL:

    My mother finds them hilarious.

MRS. CRUMP:

    That makes two people who think it's a
    comedy—your mother and Chekhov. If you ask
    me, Polina's pathetic. Throwing herself at Dr.
    What's-his-name.

PAUL:

    Dorn. And I don't think she's pathetic. She loves
    him!

MRS. CRUMP:

    The man's a scoundrel. It's obvious he's just
    using her.

MARGARET:

    We all make mistakes, don't we, Mrs. Crump?
    That's how we learn. That's how we grow.

MRS. CRUMP:

    If I had a daughter, Margaret, I'd remind her not
    to be so free with her charms. I'd tell her not to
    give herself to the first Johnny-come-lately.

MARGARET:

    But what if he's special, Mrs. Crump? What if
    he's a soul mate?

DAISY:

> Or worse, what if he's a jerk, but she can't help herself? What is she thinks of him every waking minute of every day? What if she'd sooner die than never see him again? What then?

> *Offstage, a car stops on the road.*

MRS. CRUMP:

> I can see now why Daisy wants to be an actress.

> *JACK enters the cottage.*

DAISY:

> Maggie! Look! It's Dad! He's back! ... (*Screaming, she and MARGARET rush into his arms*) Dad, I thought you'd forgotten all about us. I really did. (*She hugs him*)

JACK:

> Margaret!

MARGARET:

> We thought you were never coming back, Dad.

DAISY:

> I almost forgot what you looked like. And don't laugh.

JACK:

> I missed you, too, sweetheart. I'll never let you out of my sight again. I promise.

MRS. CRUMP:

> Hello there, Jack. Welcome home.

MARGARET:

Did you find Sally a place? Is she all settled in?

JACK:

We'll talk about Sally later. Right now I want to hear what you girls have been up to ... How were they, Mrs. Crump? They give you any trouble?

DAISY:

Trouble? Us?

MRS. CRUMP:

Not in the least, did you, girls?

DAISY:

You'll never believe this, Dad, but Maggie has a boyfriend!

MARGARET:

Daisy! ... Dad, this is Paul Wyatt. I invited Mrs. Crump and him to dinner ... Paul, this my Dad.

PAUL and JACK shake hands.

PAUL:

How do you do, sir.

JACK:

Hello, Paul ... So you and Margaret are friends, are you?

MARGARET:

Paul works at the Lodge, Dad. He's a waiter.

JACK:

A waiter?

MRS. CRUMP:

Life is full of surprises, isn't it, Jack? Like finding
half a worm in your apple.

DAISY:

Mrs. Crump!

MRS. CRUMP:

All you can do, I suppose, is roll with the
punches.

Light fades on the cottage.

NARRATOR:

Dad had a surprise of his own, but he didn't
break it to us that night. He waited till the next
morning …

That's when he sat us down on the dock and
gave us the news: he and Sally had reconciled.
Instead of separating, they'd patched things up
in Jericho, and now all four of us were to spend
the remaining weeks of the summer, the way we
used to, at Old Orchard Beach in Maine. That
day was to be our last at Willow Beach. That day
was August 2nd …

*The lights rise on the dock … MARGARET, DAISY,
and JACK are there, MARGARET standing, JACK
seated on a deck-chair, drinking. DAISY dangles her
feet off the dock.*

MARGARET:

Dad, why are you letting her do this? She's just
using you again. Can't you see that?

DAISY:

> She doesn't deserve you, Dad. She's nothing but a selfish bitch.

JACK:

> That's enough, Daisy.

MARGARET:

> She's already made you a laughingstock, her and Mr. Rush. How can you just forgive her?

JACK:

> Things are different now, Margaret. Gordon Rush moved to Texas last week. He asked for the transfer himself ... Sally seems relieved that he's gone.

DAISY:

> Dad, please.

JACK:

> She wants to make a go of it, Margaret. She told me that herself. She wants to turn over a new leaf.

DAISY:

> A new leaf? Sally?

MARGARET:

> Know what, Dad? I don't think you believe a word of it. Keep talking, you might convince yourself.

JACK:

Look, I'm not saying she's perfect. Sally has faults like anyone else. But God, Margaret, don't you think people can change?

DAISY:

Not Sally.

JACK:

You've never given her a chance, either one of you. From the first moment you met her, you kept her at arm's length. How do you think that makes her feel? Shut out like that day after day?

DAISY:

No one can take Mom's place.

JACK:

She's never tried to, Daisy, and you know it. She knows how you both feel about your mom. She respects that.

MARGARET:

Why did you marry her, Dad? Why?

JACK:

I know you don't want to hear this, you two, but maybe my feelings for Sally run deeper than you think.

MARGARET:

Dad, you've had too much bourbon.

JACK:

It's not the same as what I had with your mom, but dammit, it's just as real … Some day you'll understand.

MARGARET:

I might understand algebra some day, but I'm not holding my breath.

JACK:

Tell you one thing, Margaret. Maybe if you gave Sally the benefit of the doubt, you'd see there's more to her than meets the eye. You might even like her.

DAISY:

If she's so terrific, Dad, why did she hop into bed with Mr. Rush?

JACK:

I don't think he was ever a threat, do you, Daisy? He was more likely Sally's way of getting my attention.

DAISY:

No one ever said she was subtle, Dad.

JACK:

Alright, that's settled then. Like I told you before, we've rented the same cottage we had last summer. You girls liked it, remember? All those geraniums on the porch? The orange hammock?

MARGARET:

Dad, listen to me. I don't want to go to Maine with you and Sally. I want to stay here.

DAISY:

I want to stay with her, Dad.

JACK:

Don't talk nonsense. You're both coming with me, and that's that. I don't want to hear another word from either one of you.

MARGARET:

Dad, Daisy and I could stay with Mrs. Crump. She wouldn't mind. She likes us.

JACK:

No, I said.

MARGARET:

I can ask her right now, if you'd like. She's home.

JACK:

You aren't listening, are you? Tomorrow we're packing the car and driving to Maine. Sally's expecting us.

DAISY:

What about Tim, Dad? We're just getting to know each other ... Doesn't that matter?

MARGARET:

It's a perfect chance to have Sally all to yourself, Dad. Without Daisy and me always underfoot. Wouldn't you like that?

DAISY:

It'd be like a second honeymoon, Dad.

JACK:

Look, I'm not keeping this up till I'm blue in the face. We're leaving here tomorrow morning, and that's that. I've made up my mind. (*He picks up his chair and exits*)

DAISY:

Now what do we do?

Light fades on the dock.

Music: the hymn, 'Shall We Gather at the River'.

NARRATOR:

As soon as I could, I ran to the Lodge and told Paul to meet me at the Church on his lunch break. It was a Saturday, and the hymns from choir practice seemed to soar like doves above the white steeple.

The lights rise on the churchyard.

PAUL:

This is where we first met, remember? Seems so long ago ... You were standing here by the tree. Like that woman in the dream. That's what gave me the excuse to talk to you.

MARGARET:

Paul, I'm sorry.

PAUL:

Tell him you won't go. Tell him you don't want to.

MARGARET:

You know I can't do that.

PAUL:

I bet I could get you work at the Lodge. Mr. Morris needs some extra help. You want me to ask?

MARGARET:

Paul, I can't. It's different for you. You're older. You're on your own.

PAUL:

Well, it's bloody unfair. He just expects you to jump like a dog every time he snaps his fingers. It doesn't matter how you feel, does it?

MARGARET:

It's not as bad as all that. Look, we'll see each other in September. I know it sounds far away, but it's really not ... What would Robbie Burns say?

PAUL:

He's not much comfort.
'The soger frae the war returns
The sailor frae the main,
But I hae parted from my Love,
Never to meet again, my dear,
Never to meet again.'

MARGARET:

> (*moves into his arms*) It won't be that way, Paul.
> Not for us. I won't let it … Remember the night
> you first kissed me? The night we danced to Sam
> Cooke's 'You Send Me'?

PAUL:

> The day we first met.

MARGARET:

> Want the truth, Paul? I was so crazy about you, I
> probably would've made love right there on the
> dock, Mrs. Crump or no Mrs. Crump.

PAUL:

> Great. Now she tells me.

MARGARET:

> You said I kissed like a virgin, remember? Well,
> I've been thinking, Paul. About what you said.
> And …

PAUL:

> And?

MARGARET:

> Well, I don't want to be like that anymore. Like a
> virgin … That's what I wanted to tell you.

PAUL:

> What are you saying, Maggie? Just so there's no
> misunderstanding.

MARGARET:

> I want us to make love, Paul. I want you to be my
> first.

PAUL:

> You sure of this?

MARGARET:

> Of course I'm sure ... Tonight will be my last
> night here. I want it to be special, Paul. I want to
> remember this summer for the rest of my life.

PAUL:

> We'll both remember it, Maggie.

MARGARET:

> (*coyly*) But just so you don't think I'm easy, you
> have to answer one skill-testing question.

PAUL:

> You mean, if I know the answer, I get to ravish
> you in the churchyard? Right now? In broad
> daylight?

MARGARET:

> Not now, stupid. Tonight.

PAUL:

> I knew there was a catch ... Go on.

MARGARET:

> Well, if Babe Ruth is the Sultan of Swat, and Moe
> Soloman is the Rabbi of Swat, who is the Crown
> Prince of Swat?

PAUL:

Let's see. It can't be Ted Williams, he's the Splendid Splinter. And Mickey Mantle is the Commerce Comet. Stan Musial is the Denora Greyhound ...

MARGARET:

Paul!

PAUL:

Alright—Lou Gehrig.

MARGARET:

Lucky guess. (*They kiss*)

Light fades on the churchyard.

NARRATOR:

That afternoon, Daisy decided to seek Mrs. Crump's help in winning back Tim. Since we were leaving the next morning, there wasn't much time. Mrs. Crump had many tricks up her sleeve. Many ways of making a young girl irresistible ... Like the apple of love, for instance.

The lights rise on the yard ... JACK sits in a folding chair, reading Life *magazine. MRS. CRUMP and DAISY are in conversation, DAISY taking notes.*

MRS. CRUMP:

First off, you go into an orchard just before sunrise and pick an apple. Not just any apple, either. Has to be the most beautiful apple on the tree.

DAISY:

I don't have time to be fussy, Mrs. Crump. We're getting an early start, remember?

JACK:

She's only seeing Tim for a few minutes tonight. That is, if she can find him.

MRS. CRUMP:

In that case, use a store-bought apple. The spell won't be as strong, that's all.

DAISY:

Then what?

MRS. CRUMP:

Then write your name and Tim's on a piece of white paper—in blood.

JACK:

Mrs. Crump.

MRS. CRUMP:

I'm only telling her what to do, Jack. She doesn't have to do it ... (*To DAISY*) Next, take a second piece of paper and write the word 'FOREVER' on it. In capital letters.

DAISY:

FOREVER?

MRS. CRUMP:

FOREVER ... Place the two pieces of paper face to face, roll them together, and tie the roll with three hairs from your head and three hairs from Tim's.

DAISY:

Where am I supposed to get three hairs from Tim's head?

JACK:

Ask to use his pocket comb.

MRS. CRUMP:

Next, cut the apple in two, remove the core, and fold in the paper. Then you join the two halves together with a rusty nail.

JACK:

A rusty nail?

DAISY:

Have you ever seen this work, Mrs. Crump? Even once?

MRS. CRUMP:

I'm not finished yet ... Dry the apple in the oven, then wrap it in laurel and myrtle leaves.

DAISY:

Oh, right. I just happen to have laurel and myrtle leaves.

MRS. CRUMP:

Lastly, you slip the apple of love under Tim's bed. Then you wait.

JACK:

How does she go about that, Mrs. Crump?
Slipping the apple of love under Tim's bed?

MRS. CRUMP:

That's up to her, Jack. I only know the steps to
follow. (*To DAISY*) But just you watch, luv. In no
time flat, he'll be prancing under your window,
an orchid in one hand, his heart in the other.

MARGARET enters, carrying the whiskey bottle.

MARGARET:

I don't know, Mrs. Crump. All that sounds pretty
complicated to me. Doesn't it to you, Dad? ...
(*She pours whiskey into JACK's glass*)

NARRATOR:

I thought I was being so clever, pouring Dad
drinks. A few more, and he'd be out for the
night. Then I could make my escape to the
churchyard, and the long night ahead.

MARGARET:

Dad, why don't you tell Mrs. Crump how you and
Mom first got together. Bet she'd find it amusing.

JACK:

Mrs. Crump doesn't want to hear that, Margaret.

MRS. CRUMP:

Why don't you let Mrs. Crump be the judge of
that?

DAISY:

>Well, I'd like to hear it again … It was Babe Ruth who lit a fire under you, wasn't it, Dad?

JACK:

>Sure was.

MRS. CRUMP:

>The baseball player?

JACK:

>That was 1935, the year the Detroit Tigers won the World Series.

MARGARET:

>Dad tried out for the Boston Braves that year, Mrs. Crump. That's how he met the Bambino. The Yankees had dropped Ruth in February, after 21 seasons. Imagine: the Sultan of Swat. 714 home runs.

JACK:

>To me, the Babe *was* baseball. He also liked bridge, cigars, kids, Seagram's whiskey, and women.

DAISY:

>Especially women.

JACK:

>One day, he nudges me in the dug-out. He was terrible with names. Couldn't remember names or faces to save himself … 'Kid,' he says, 'you see that little gal over there by the fence? The one who can't keep her eyes off you?' And he spat

some tobacco juice. 'Well, let me tell you, kid. That's one helluva nice-looking gal, and if you don't hurry up and say hello to her, by God, I will.'

MARGARET:

Dad had noticed her before. He just didn't have the nerve to do anything.

DAISY:

The Babe scared you spitless, didn't he, Dad? You thought he was serious.

JACK:

Sure did ... After the game, I walked straight to your mom and introduced myself. Asked her if she'd have dinner with me ... So you see, Mrs. Crump, if it hadn't been for George Herman Ruth, these two wouldn't be here today, pestering us both half to death.

DAISY:

Times were simpler then, Dad. Life's not like that anymore.

MRS. CRUMP:

Life's what you make of it, Daisy ... But look, if the apple of love's not suitable, I have just the thing. Take a small piece of red cloth and lock yourself in a dark room.

DAISY:

Red cloth. A dark room.

MRS. CRUMP:

Sit there and imagine Tim's face. While you're doing that, draw a heart on the cloth.

DAISY:

This is a lot easier, Mrs. Crump.

MRS. CRUMP:

Finally, roll the red cloth into a ball and tuck it into your left armpit. Keep it there the whole time you're with him tonight. Think you can remember that?

DAISY:

It's burned into my brain … Thanks, Mrs. Crump. I'll let you know what happens. (*She hugs her*)

MRS. CRUMP:

You do that, luv.

> *DAISY, excited, exits.*

JACK:

(*rises*) Think I'll go inside. It's getting chilly out here … (*To MRS. CRUMP*) Suppose we'll see you in the morning. The girls will want to say goodbye.

MRS. CRUMP:

They could stay with me, you know, Jack. It wouldn't put me out one bit. There's plenty of room.

MARGARET:

And I didn't tell her to say that, Dad.

MRS. CRUMP:

They'd be perfectly safe here. I could put them
on the train when the time comes. They're old
enough now to travel by themselves.

JACK:

I want the girls in Maine for the month of
August. So does Sally.

MARGARET:

Dad, we've never been on a train before, Daisy
and me. It'd be fun.

JACK:

Forget it, I said.

MRS. CRUMP:

Alright, Jack, you're the boss. I'm sure both you
and Sally know what you're doing.

JACK:

Does anyone ever know? ... Someone once asked
the Babe for his theory of hitting. He said, 'I just
hit what they throw me.' Life's a lot like that,
don't you think? ... (*He exits*)

MRS. CRUMP:

(*beat*) Well, I tried.

MARGARET:

I know. Thanks, anyway.

MRS. CRUMP:

And don't ever tell your Dad about that spell I
gave you and Paul. He'd have a stroke.

MARGARET.

I won't. I promise … I'm glad you're on our side now, Mrs. Crump.

MRS. CRUMP:

Maybe Paul just needed to meet the right girl.

Pause.

MRS. CRUMP:

A penny for your thoughts, luv.

MARGARET:

I don't know. I guess I was thinking of the summer. How wonderful it's been. I met you. I met Paul … Are all summers special like this?

MRS. CRUMP:

All time is special, Margaret. There's so little of it … As for people … Well, there are those who simply fade from memory. And those that become a part of us forever.

MARGARET:

Like you and Matthew?

MRS. CRUMP:

Yes, like Matt and me … For years, you know, I dreamt of him. Even after he died, I kept his picture under my pillow. That's supposed to make you dream of the person in the photo … The last time he appeared in my dreams was many years ago. The last time, that is, till just the other night.

MARGARET:

You dreamt of him again?

MRS. CRUMP:

I saw him so clearly, too. He was waving to me
from across a shining river. It was such a lovely
dream, and I woke up so happy.

Light fades on the yard.

DAISY:

See you later, alligator.

MARGARET:

In a while, crocodile.

NARRATOR:

So, Daisy ran off to look for Tim, the ball of red
cloth tucked next to her heart. I waited till Dad
had passed out ... The full moon was shining,
and I ran up the road in its light, so excited I
thought I'd die, up toward the church, its white
steeple rising above the black trees.

Music: 'Sleep Walk' by Santo & Johnny.

NARRATOR:

As I approached the churchyard, I could see
Paul's old Buick parked beside the fence. I could
hear 'Sleep Walk' playing softly on the car radio.

*The lights rise on the churchyard ... PAUL waits
beside the white birch. MARGARET runs on, and
for a moment, they take each other in.*

PAUL:

Gosh, you look lovely.

MARGARET:

I do? I almost forgot to brush my hair ... I didn't think Dad would ever pass out.

PAUL:

I thought maybe you wouldn't show up.

MARGARET:

I thought you wouldn't.

PAUL:

Are you kidding? I've already carved our initials in the tree. Just the way you asked me to.

MARGARET:

It's perfect, Paul. The birch is young. The knife is new ... Know what we're supposed to do next?

PAUL:

What?

MARGARET:

We're supposed to bury the knife under the tree. Then make love on that exact spot.

PAUL:

Sounds like an excellent idea to me.

MARGARET:

Mrs. Crump says if you follow all four steps, our love will last a long, long time. Maybe forever. Oh Paul, I'm so happy.

PAUL:

Are you, Maggie?

They kiss.

MARGARET:

Look, Paul! Look! (*She points at the sky*) Isn't that Sputnik?

PAUL:

Sputnik? Where?

MARGARET:

There. It's almost over the church. A pinpoint of white light. Look how it's moving among the stars.

PAUL:

150 miles up. 18,000 miles an hour.

MARGARET:

Doesn't seem to be moving fast at all, does it?

PAUL:

Orbits the earth every 96 minutes.

MARGARET:

It's like an omen, Paul. I know it.

PAUL:

You're beginning to sound like Mrs. Crump.

MARGARET:

Remember that night on the dock? You said the world we live in had changed ... I believe you now, Paul. Suddenly the world seems as new to me as that moon up there. Bright and shiny, like a new dime.

PAUL:

'It is the moon, I ken her horn,
That's blinkin' in the lift sae hae;
She shines sae bright to wyle us hame,
But, by my sooth! She'll wait a wee.'

MARGARET removes the ring MRS. CRUMP gave her.

Light fades on the churchyard.

NARRATOR:

That night, Paul and I made love. Right on the spot he'd buried the pocket knife. Then he found a Jack Scott song on the car radio, and we danced. Afterwards, we drove his Buick all around Wolf Lake, each taking turns at the wheel. We even took our clothes off and drove naked for miles, singing along to 'Rock Around The Clock' and 'Bye, Bye, Love', the lake shining beside us like a promise. It was the freest moment of my life. Nothing before or since has even come close, the fields and orchards flashing by, the music loud and so familiar, the white road ahead like life itself, stretching far, far into the distance ... Yes, Henry James thought 'summer afternoon' the two most beautiful words in English. But, for me, the most beautiful have always been 'I remember'. The most beautiful, and often, of course, the most painful ...

DAISY:

    (*off*) Stop it, Tim! Don't!

    The lights rise on the cottage ... MARGARET bursts
    in from outside.

MARGARET:

    Dad! Dad, wake up! Daisy and Tim are out on
    the lake! The boat just tipped over! ... Dad! Get
    up! Get up! Something terrible has happened!
    Please, God! No! No! Please! Please! Not Daisy!
    Not my sister! ...

    She dashes outside and down to the dock.

    Light fades on the cottage.

NARRATOR:

    Paul had just dropped me off, when I heard the
    noise out on the lake. Later, Tim said that Daisy
    had stood up in the boat. Maybe she had,
    considering what happened the last time they
    were out there ... After I tried to wake my dad, I
    ran back to the dock. But I couldn't swim, you
    see. All I could do was stand there, helpless, the
    most helpless I've ever been in my life.

    A light on the dock. MARGARET and the
    NARRATOR stand side by side.

MARGARET:

    Daisy! Daisy, can you hear me? Daisy! ... Please,
    God! Please, help my sister! Please, don't let her
    die! Please!

NARRATOR:

And then it happened. Suddenly, out of
nowhere, Mrs. Crump appeared. Maybe she'd
heard me screaming. Or maybe she'd seen it all
from her cottage. I don't know. I only know that
suddenly she came sweeping down the lawn, her
bare feet slapping on the weathered planks of
the dock. I saw her spring silently past me, almost
in slow motion, her long flannel nightgown white
in the moonlight, then ballooning as it filled with
water ... And then she was swimming as hard as
she could, striking out toward the capsized boat.
At first I could see her begin to tire, then
struggle, and finally ... finally I saw her go under.
She wasn't in the greatest shape, Mrs. Crump.
And the flannel nightgown, I suppose, just
became too heavy ... The second time she went
down, she never came up, except for one pale
hand. I could see it in the slash of moonlight.
Her fingers seemed to scratch at the sky. And it
looked to me then, as it still looks in memory,
just as though she were waving ... (*She's overcome
by emotion*)

> *Music: a few bars of 'Blessed Assurance', very
> faint, as though it still lingers in the NARRATOR's
> memory.*

> *Finally, the NARRATOR and MARGARET turn and
> face one another. They embrace. It is as though the
> NARRATOR, at last, is able to forgive her younger
> self ... Then MARGARET exits.*

CAITLIN enters, carrying roses.

CAITLIN:

Hi, Gran. Looks like it might not storm after all. See? The sky's clearing up across the lake.

NARRATOR:

MacGregor's Island seems close enough to touch doesn't it?

CAITLIN:

I was up at the church just now. The minister said you'd already dropped by ... He gave me these roses for Mrs. Crump.

NARRATOR:

Don't suppose you know who he is, do you, Caitlin?

CAITLIN:

The minister? No.

NARRATOR:

Why, that's Tim Scott, Daisy's old boyfriend. Became a minister not long after his father died ... Bet he even knows John 3:16 now.

CAITLIN:

... This is where it happened, isn't it, Gran? Just off this dock.

NARRATOR:

Yes, the water's quite deep out there. And, of course, it was night ... Somehow Daisy had struck her head on the boat. Tim kept diving, but he couldn't locate her in the dark.

CAITLIN:

They found her body the next day, didn't they, Gran? Not far from Mrs. Crump.

NARRATOR:

(*nods*) Later, my Dad gave me the piece of red satin they found inside her dress—still with the heart drawn on it. He also gave me a talisman Mrs. Crump had given her. Daisy had worn it around her neck. An old French sou with a hole punched in the centre ...

Pause.

CAITLIN:

Gran, I have a confession to make. It wasn't just idle curiosity that made me want to come here. Maybe you'd already guessed that.

NARRATOR:

I think I had, darling.

CAITLIN:

I was hoping you'd find something here, Gran. Some sort of comfort.

NARRATOR:

How wise you are, kiddo.

CAITLIN:

Sooner or later, you know, you have to forgive yourself. The way people do in those books you write.

NARRATOR:

Maybe I'm beginning to, Caitlin.

CAITLIN:

Know what I think you always seem to forget? How young you were.

NARRATOR:

Yes, we weren't much older than you, were we? Just kids. Paul. Daisy. Myself.

CAITLIN:

Besides, Daisy wouldn't want you to go on blaming yourself. You know she wouldn't.

NARRATOR:

Oh, Caitlin, did you read what was written on the sundial? (*CAITLIN shakes her head*) 'Time heals all but memory'. (*To the audience*) We buried Daisy in the Congregational Church cemetery in Jericho. Buried her beside my mom, on a lovely Tuesday afternoon. Tim and his dad came down for the funeral ... (*DAISY and JACK appear on stage, DAISY sitting on the dock, dangling her feet in the water*)

Music: 'My True Love' by Jack Scott.

126

NARRATOR:

As for Paul and me,—(*MARGARET and PAUL appear in the churchyard, dancing to the song on the car radio*)—well, we never saw each other again, not after Willow Beach. It wasn't his fault. He kept calling me in Vermont, but I wouldn't answer. You see, I didn't think I deserved to be happy, not for a very long time ... Daisy's death had come between us ... had ripped the flower up by its roots ...

JACK:

(*to the audience*) Later, when Margaret found out she was pregnant, she decided to keep the baby, which was something a single girl didn't do back then. Sally and I insisted she give it up. But instead she ran off to New York City, worked in a folk club, had my grandson, and raised him on her own. In the summer of '69 she even took him to Woodstock ...

NARRATOR:

And Dad ... Well, after Daisy drowned, Dad hit rock bottom as hard as any man I've ever seen. It was Sally who talked him into AA. They're quite a stuffy couple now, still living in Jericho, in the house with the cherry tree ... (*MRS. CRUMP appears in the yard*) ... As for Mrs. Crump, I keep a framed black-and-white photo of her from that summer, her eyes smiling beneath the brim of her straw hat, a twist of cigar smoke in the air. It sits on my mantlepiece in Burlington. And people who visit say 'Who's that woman,

Margaret? She looks so outrageous.' And I say,
'That woman? Why, that woman is Mrs. Crump,
of course. My hero' ... I still can't seem to call
her Kathleen.

*CAITLIN walks to MRS. CRUMP's grave, sets down
the roses.*

NARRATOR:
(*the first four lines to the audience, the rest to
CAITLIN*)
'That year, snow came in April and again
In May, and the pony died in his harness
But in summer, under the whitewashed trees,
A girl in a white dress gave me an apple.
I fitted my teeth in the marks her teeth
Had made; so we were one. Then dusk
Moved slowly among the trees like a blue
Smoke at night, and I cried that joy
Could come so easily, for then I knew
It must break with as little warning.'

*The NARRATOR and CAITLIN embrace, becoming
part of the tableau.*

Blackout.